# Gingerbread

## Victoria Blakemore

In loving memory of Thomas and Isabella Blakemore

Copyright info/picture credits

# Table of Contents

# What is Gingerbread?

When many people think of gingerbread, they think of decorated houses and gingerbread men.

The word actually means any kind of baked good that is made with molasses and ginger.

Gingerbread men, houses, and

trees are common treats around

Christmas.

# Ingredients

Recipes for gingerbread can have different **ingredients**.

Some ingredients that are in many recipes are flour, eggs, molasses, butter, and ginger. They may also have other spices like cinnamon, nutmeg, cloves, and allspice.

After the gingerbread dough

is mixed and rolled out,

cookie cutters can be used

to make different shapes.

# Ginger

The ginger spice used in gingerbread comes from the root of the ginger plant. The roots are dried and used for cooking.

The ginger plant originally came from Southeast Asia. It has been used in food and medicine there for many years.

Ginger root is often used in soups, sauces, baked goods, and even tea. It is said to have many health benefits.

# Molasses

Molasses is a sweetener. It is usually made from sugarcane when it is **refined** into sugar. It is often in the form of a dark, sticky syrup.

Molasses syrup has many uses. It can be used to make brown sugar, for baking, and even for natural **remedies**.

Molasses is higher in nutrients

than other sweeteners. It is

also lower in sugar.

# History

The first recipe for gingerbread is believed to have come from ancient Greece thousands of years ago. There are also recipes from China around the same time.

By the early 1100's, it was becoming popular in parts of Europe.

Recipes for gingerbread may have been brought to the rest of Europe by the **crusaders**.

# Gingerbread Fairs

Gingerbread fairs were very popular in the 1600's and 1700's. People would travel from far away to go to the fair.

Many treats and decorations made with gingerbread were sold at gingerbread fairs.

Treats like these are made at fairs

in Germany. They are decorated

with frosting and hung on ribbons.

Gingerbread treats were dusted with powdered sugar. They were also sometimes decorated with foil or gold leaf. Details could be carved into the treats.

The cookies that were made with gingerbread would be shaped to match the season.

They could be shaped like flowers in the spring, animals in the autumn, and stars in the winter.

# Guilds

In the 1600's, making gingerbread was a special job. In some places, only certain people were allowed to make gingerbread to sell.

These people were members of special **guilds**. They were specially trained to make gingerbread.

At the time, making

gingerbread was thought to

be a special kind of art.

# Gingerbread Men

Queen Elizabeth I of England came up with the idea of gingerbread men. She had them made to look like important people who came to see her.

Queen Elizabeth was so fond of gingerbread that she had someone whose only job was to make it.

Now, gingerbread men are a

very common treat. They are

decorated with icing and candy.

# Gingerbread Houses

Gingerbread houses were first made in Germany in the 1700's. The idea may have come from the story of Hansel and Gretel.

The pieces of gingerbread are put together with icing. As it hardens, it holds the pieces together.

20

Once the house is put together, it is decorated with icing and candies. The icing helps to hold the pieces on.

# Ornaments

Some people use gingerbread to make ornaments for their Christmas tree.

The dough is made into shapes first. Then, a hole is poked through each one before they are baked. After they are baked, they are decorated and a ribbon is added.

Gingerbread is hard enough to

be hung up as ornaments. The

ginger in the dough helps to

**preserve** the cookies.

# In Literature

Gingerbread has been used in stories for many years. The house that Hansel and Gretel find in the woods is a gingerbread house in some stories.

Many stories are written about gingerbread men. In these stories, the gingerbread man comes to life after he is baked.

He often runs away and is chased

by people and animals who want

to eat him.

# Nutrition

Gingerbread can be high in calories because of the sugar and fat it contains.

However, it is also full of many nutrients. It has lots of iron, magnesium, and vitamins. They can help your body to stay healthy.

Even with those nutrients, gingerbread is not the healthiest treat. It should be eaten in **moderation**.

# Health Benefits

The iron and magnesium in gingerbread can help to keep your heart and blood healthy.

The main part of gingerbread that helps your body is the ginger. It can help to settle an upset stomach and help to keep you from getting sick.

Ginger can also help to lessen pain.

Some researchers believe that it

can even help to fight cancer.

# Gingerbread at Christmas

Gingerbread is often made when it gets close to Christmas. This probably started because people long ago believed that the spices in gingerbread could keep you warm.

Now, making gingerbread at Christmas is more of a **tradition**.

Some families make gingerbread cookies each year. People also make and decorate gingerbread houses with their families.

Some people enter contests to see who can make the most beautiful gingerbread house.

Gingerbread is an important **tradition** in many families all over the world.

# Glossary

**Crusaders:** people who fought in the Crusades in Europe and Asia

**Guilds**: a group of people who had the same job and worked together to protect their interests

**Ingredients**: parts of a mixture

**Moderation**: not having too much

**Preserve**: to keep something from going bad

**Refine**: to make pure

**Remedy**: something used to take

away pain or heal a sickness

**Tradition**: a custom that is handed

down in a family or group of people

# About the Author

Victoria Blakemore is a first grade

teacher in Southwest Florida with a

passion for reading.

You can visit her at

www.elementaryexplorers.com

# Also in This Series

| | | | | | | |
|---|---|---|---|---|---|---|
| ray Wolves | Sloths | Flamingos | Camels | Koalas | Honey Bees | Pandas |
| Pangolins | White-Tailed Deer | Orcas | Giraffes | Corn | Meerkats | Echidnas |
| Walruses | Raccoons | Bald Eagles | Apples | Arctic Foxes | Red Pandas | Cassowaries |
| Tigers | Ladybugs | Moose | Beluga Whales | Leopards | Elephants | Jellyfish |
| Binturongs | Lions | Dolphins | Reindeer | Hammerhead Sharks | Hippos | Pumpkins |
| Peafowl | Chameleons | Florida Panthers | Aye-Ayes | Black Bears | Cheetahs | Manatees |
| Gingerbread | Polar Bears | Hot Chocolate | Orangutans | Coyotes | Marshmallows | Strawberries |

# Also in This Series

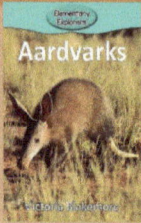

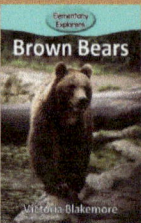

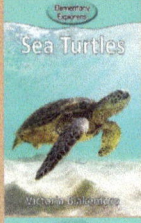

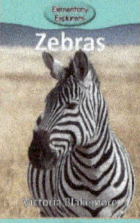

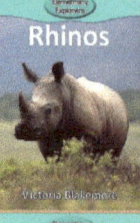

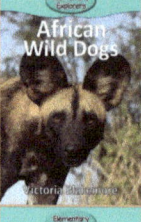

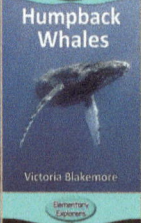

Aardvarks — Victoria Blakemore
Mako Sharks — Victoria Blakemore
Alligators — Victoria Blakemore
Frogs — Victoria Blakemore
Hedgehogs — Victoria Blakemore
Brown Bears — Victoria Blakemore
Bongos — Victoria Blakemore

Sea Turtles — Victoria Blakemore
Quokkas — Victoria Blakemore
Muskrats — Victoria Blakemore
Zebras — Victoria Blakemore
Red Foxes — Victoria Blakemore
Ring-Tailed Lemurs — Victoria Blakemore
Platypuses — Victoria Blakemore

Anteaters — Victoria Blakemore
Kangaroos — Victoria Blakemore
Rhinos — Victoria Blakemore
Jaguars — Victoria Blakemore
Wombats — Victoria Blakemore
Capybaras — Victoria Blakemore
Gorillas — Victoria Blakemore

Cats — Victoria Blakemore
Skunks — Victoria Blakemore
Butterflies — Victoria Blakemore
Dingoes — Victoria Blakemore
Snow Leopards — Victoria Blakemore
African Wild Dogs — Victoria Blakemore
Penguins — Victoria Blakemore

Whale Sharks — Victoria Blakemore
Wolverines — Victoria Blakemore
Warthogs — Victoria Blakemore
Caracals — Victoria Blakemore
Badgers — Victoria Blakemore
Seals — Victoria Blakemore
Hummingbird — Victoria Blakemore

Pikas — Victoria Blakemore
Humpback Whales — Victoria Blakemore
Pumas — Victoria Blakemore
Lemonade — Victoria Blakemore
Llamas — Victoria Blakemore
Tulips — Victoria Blakemore
Ostriches — Victoria Blakemore

Sunflowers — Victoria Blakemore
Fennec Foxes — Victoria Blakemore
Sea Lions — Victoria Blakemore
Squirrels — Victoria Blakemore
Roses — Victoria Blakemore
Porcupines — Victoria Blakemore
Ice Cream — Victoria Blakemore

www.ingramcontent.com/pod-product-compliance
Lightning Source LLC
Chambersburg PA
CBHW051251020426
42333CB00025B/3162